STAFFC
Ghost

Prepare to be frightened by these terrifying tales
from around Staffordshire

By

David Bell

BRADWELL
BOOKS

Published by Bradwell Books
9 Orgreave Close Sheffield S13 9NP

Email: books@bradwellbooks.co.uk
© David Bell 2014

British Library Cataloguing in Publication Data: a catalogue
record for this book is available from the British Library.

1st Edition

ISBN: 9781902674988

Design by: jenksdesign@yahoo.co.uk

CONTENTS

Ghosts of Tutbury Castle   7

The gypsy's curse: Alton Towers   10

Buried alive: Stone and Rushton Spencer   13

The rector's widow: Checkley   17

Ghosts of Uttoxeter   20

Lud's church   22

The girl in Brough Park: Leek   28

The Mermaid's Pool: Thorncliffe   30

The highland drummer boy: Tompkin   32

Red stockings: Wetwood   34

Molly Leigh: Burslem   37

Ghost in a police hostel: Baswich   41

Mysteries of the shepherd's monument: Shugborough   44

The bloody steps: Rugeley   48

The skeleton tree: Hednesford   53

The horn dance: Abbots Bromley   56

The laughing cavalier and entombed Elspeth: Lichfield   61

A last visit from a friend: Elford   65

The ghost that only children can see: Hopwas   68

Ghosts of Tamworth Castle   71

Sinai house: Shobnall   75

INTRODUCTION

Staffordshire is a very varied county, stretching from the borders of Birmingham and the Black Country in the south to the moorlands of Leek and Biddulph in the north. The county has many places with ghostly reputations. Some are in areas where you might expect hauntings. The castle at Tamworth and the castle ruins at Tutbury each have a large number of ghostly residents. Alton Towers has many legends connected with a gypsy curse that dates from an event there in the 1770s.

There are tales connected with graves in Burslem and Rushton Spencer. But there are more surprising locations: a haunted former police headquarters at Baswich, an oak tree on Cannock Chase, and a set of canal steps in Rugeley. There is the macabre account from Tompkin, which explains how the village got its name. There are strange stories about the 11th-century reindeer horns that hang in Abbots Bromley church, and which are used in the annual horn dance. There is a terrifying tale of the young stable boy buried alive by the apothecary of Stone, just to save the social standing of his daughter.

Lichfield ghosts include the Laughing Cavalier – always cheerful despite his fatal wounds – and the heartbreaking story of a young girl trapped in a subterranean tunnel under the city streets. The widow of the rector of Checkley – a formidable and judgemental woman in her lifetime – still haunts the rectory and the church grounds, making her strict moral disapproval known to the residents. Another rectory, this time in Elford, was where the rector saw the figure of a friend, only to hear later that the friend had just died.

The enigmatic Shepherd's Monument in the grounds of Shugborough Hall has attracted people over the centuries, anxious to solve its secrets and mysteries. Add in Lud's Church – not a building but a cleft in the earth and the most mysterious location in the whole county – and you will see that Staffordshire has a rich and varied heritage of places for the ghost hunter to visit.

David Bell

GHOSTS OF TUTBURY CASTLE

Tutbury Castle was built in 1071, as one of the new castles built to stamp the authority of the Norman conquerors. It was the home of the de Ferrers family, and later of the earls of Lancaster. It was destroyed and rebuilt several times. The present ruins date from the 14th century, although the chapel ruins are older and are from the 12th century.

Tutbury Castle.
© *Shutterstock/Arena Photo UK*

When Barry Vallens became the custodian of Tutbury Castle in 1977, he experienced a number of the castle's ghosts. The first one he saw was that of a monk. One of Barry's first tasks was to clear out the overgrown and rubbish-filled dry ditch that once served as a moat. As he looked up he saw a robed figure standing on the bank. Barry climbed up towards it but it vanished. He saw the same figure a few weeks later in another part of the ditch, and this time he could see the face of the monk. Again the figure disappeared before his eyes. 'There is no way the monk the monk could have left the location without passing me,' he told me.

Both of these sightings were in an area known as the vinecroft, where in former times the monks from the nearby Cistercian abbey used to grow hops for making ale. Barry wonders if the ghost is that of a monk who worked at growing the hops, though he is puzzled as to why the ghost was in a brown robe, as the Cistercian monks usually wore black.

Another ghost at the castle is that of the 'White Lady' who haunts the watchtower. Many people claim she is the ghost of Mary, Queen of Scots, who was a guest/prisoner at Tutbury Castle from 1569 to 70 and again in 1585–6.

Barry, however, is convinced it is the ghosts of a Lady Marlborough, who was killed there in peculiar circumstances. She used the tower as a secret rendezvous for meeting her lover, but was slain there by the castle steward. The steward claimed that she rushed at him and impaled herself on his drawn sword, but the steward was immediately killed by Lord Marlborough. It is possible to speculate whether Lord Marlborough had ordered the steward to kill his unfaithful wife, then killed the man to ensure his silence.

This ghost has been sighted by many visitors to the castle, including a young, tearful schoolgirl visiting Tutbury for the first time, who knew nothing of the White Lady story. Barry saw the girl crying, and asked her teacher what was the trouble. 'She's just being silly,' the teacher said. 'She says she saw a lady in white up in the watchtower.' Barry then told the unbelieving teacher the legend of the ghost of Lady Marlborough.

There is also the ghost of a Norman knight, whom Barry describes as 'a frightful fellow'. He may be a member of the Ferrers family, who were given Tutbury Castle by William the Conqueror. He is buried in the chapel ruins in the centre castle. This ghost seems to make it his mission to drive visitors away from the castle.

Barry once found a silver and ivory glove ring in the chapel ruins and took it to his rooms to clean it up. He and his wife then suffered a series of supernatural events, including a disembodied hand tapping on the window, until the ring was returned to the chapel.

Barry told me that in his first six months as custodian, the place seemed to be testing him. 'This place takes you over,' he said. 'I had to make sure it didn't dominate me.' He then added, 'You have to learn to work with it, or everything goes wrong.'

THE GYPSY'S CURSE: Alton Towers

Two stories from Alton Towers both concern gypsies – one a ghost – seen at or near the stately home. In 1848, Dr F. A. Paley was riding back to the Towers with a 15-year-old boy, Bertram, the nephew of the Earl of Shrewsbury. The Earl was a staunch Roman Catholic and Bertram was his heir. He was keen that Bertram should inherit the title, as the next relations were Protestant cousins. Dr Paley was engaged as the boy's tutor.

As Bertram and his tutor were riding along a river bank, Dr Paley spotted on the wooded slope a gypsy woman in a clearing. He couldn't work out how she had got to such a difficult spot, so he dismounted and handed the reins to his pupil. He clambered up the steep, boulder-strewn slope through the trees, but as he approached the gypsy she disappeared. Puzzled he climbed down again, and after checking that Bertram had seen the woman too, he remounted and the two continued their journey up to Alton Towers.

As they arrived, they were met by the Countess, and Dr Paley began to recount the story about the woman he'd just seen. As soon as he mentioned the word gypsy, the Countess went pale and rushed off to her room. She failed to come to dinner that evening. Later the resident family chaplain took the tutor aside and reprimanded him for causing distress to the Countess, 'because of the legend'. Dr Paley knew nothing of any legend, but the priest explained that there was a belief that if a gypsy was seen near Alton Towers, a member of the family would die.

Sadly the legend proved correct, because a few months later Bertram – who had seemed a healthy young man – caught consumption and died.

The legend about Alton Towers and the presence of gypsies began some seventy years earlier. The then Earl had made substantial alterations to the Towers, including the building of a new ballroom. When it was completed, he invited members of the nobility from miles around – some even from abroad – to attend a week of celebrations.

Alton Towers

On the final evening, a ball was held in the new ballroom. Everyone was dancing and enjoying themselves, when suddenly the music stopped and all the dancers drew back.

There in the centre of the floor was a gypsy. He was an old man with a nut-brown face, long white hair and piercing blue eyes. The Earl demanded to know who he was, how he'd got there and what on earth he wanted. The gypsy replied that in return for a small coin from each, he would like to tell the fortune of all the guests. The Earl would hear no more of it and ordered the servants to throw him out. However, at the door the gypsy shook himself free and addressed the Earl directly. He told him that he was putting a curse on his family. Referring to the oak tree that stood outside, he said that any time a branch of the tree fell, a branch of the Earl's family would die out.

That night, after all the revelries had finished, the Earl could not sleep for thinking about what the gypsy had predicted. The next morning, he ordered his gardeners to bind strong chains around the branches of the tree, so that even if one of the branches became weakened, it couldn't fall.

He had solved the immediate problem, but the legend obviously remained. Future members of the family still feared that the presence of a gypsy would presage the death of a family member.

The chained oak tree can still be seen in the grounds of Alton Towers.

BURIED ALIVE: Stone and Rushton Spencer

Tom Meaykin was born and brought up in the moorland village of Rushton Spencer, but moved twenty miles south to the town of Stone to find work. He became a servant in the household of the town apothecary, with responsibility for looking after his horses.

He was a good-looking young man and he worked hard. He made many friends in Stone and was a popular lad. However, he did encounter a serious dilemma. A pretty young lady took a fancy to him, and she 'set her cap at him'. She was determined to make him fall in love with her. This may not sound much of a problem, but the young lady in question was the daughter of his employer, the apothecary.

Everyone in Stone was highly amused by this, but when Tom's employer heard about his daughter's infatuation, he was outraged. Tom was a servant; far too lowly for his daughter. However, when he told his daughter that she was to have no more to with the stable boy, she defied her father, saying that one day she would marry Tom Meaykin.

The apothecary's social problem remained, until one day it resolved itself. Although he had been a fit and healthy lad, young Tom Meaykin suddenly dropped dead. His employer quickly had him buried in St Michael's churchyard in Stone. His daughter was heartbroken, but her father's social standing was restored.

One of the horses Tom had looked after got into the churchyard several times, and was seen pawing at Tom's grave. When Tom's ghost began to be seen wandering about the churchyard in the winter of 1781, the townspeople began to speculate whether the apothecary had in fact killed the boy. After the ghost had been observed on numerous occasions over a period of eight months, the body was exhumed. The coffin was dug up and opened. A horrifying and macabre sight met the eyes of the men who were present. Although Tom had been buried in the usual position – on his back with his arms crossed on his chest – the body in the coffin was now lying face down.

The implication was obvious. When Tom Meaykin had been buried he was not really dead but had been rendered into a state of paralysis, in which he couldn't move or speak. After the burial, he had come round in his coffin, under six feet of earth, and in his panic and terror he had managed to turn over. Tongues began to wag. Wasn't it convenient for the apothecary that his social problem had been sorted out by the boy's death? The apothecary had a motive for killing him, and no doubt he had the means at his disposal to paralyse the boy with drugs. Most of the town was convinced that the girl's father had done the terrible deed, but nothing came of it. The evidence was all circumstantial, and moreover the man was of good social standing in Stone, a man of some importance.

Tom's body was transported back to his native village, and his tomb is in the churchyard of St Lawrence in Rushton Spencer. On his gravestone, his tragic story is remembered with words referring to his 'death by violence caused by the wickedness of men'.

Rushton Spencer church

**Memento Mori
Thomas Son of Thomas
and Mary MEAYKIN
Interred July the 16 1781
Aged 21 years**

**As man falleth before
wicked men: so fell I.
Biathanatos!**

This time, Tom's body was buried the wrong way round, with his head to the west and his feet to the east, in order to lay his ghost. But the ploy has not worked. His ghost has been seen

The tombstone on Tom Meaykin's grave.

in recent years near his second burial place in Rushton Spencer, bemoaning the fact that his murderer – the apothecary of Stone – escaped without punishment.

THE RECTOR'S WIDOW: Checkley

Mrs Hutchinson, the widow of the Revd William Hutchinson, was known as a bit of a dragon during her lifetime. Following her death in 1895, her ghost appears to have maintained her reputation as a tartar and an interfering busybody.

She became a widow in 1878, and for the next seventeen years she kept a stern and unsmiling eye on village activities. Most of the villagers regarded the widow with trepidation; she was not a woman to get on the wrong side of. If anyone failed to turn up at church on a Sunday, they knew that Mrs Hutchinson would soon be knocking on their door to ask their reason. If their excuse was not compelling enough, she would give them a ferocious admonishment. She continued to rule Checkley with a rod of iron. She had a particular loathing for two young ladies who used to ride their horses through the churchyard, and she made her feelings about them very clear.

Death did nothing to diminish her vigilance. When a young clergyman, the Revd Ralph Phillips, moved into the rectory in the 1940s, he decided to hold a housewarming party. The ghost of Mrs Hutchinson was obviously not amused. Some of the house guests were staying overnight, and one of them noticed that his bedroom had no clock. He went down to get his watch from his coat pocket, but on his way back up the stairs, he met a stern-looking woman in a long black frock and a mob cap. He assumed she was a fellow guest and wished her goodnight. The woman did not reply and gave him a disapproving look. The next morning he looked round, but could not see the lady among the guests. He asked the young vicar if there were any other guests but was told that there were not. When he described the cross-looking lady on the stairs, Ralph told him that he had met the redoubtable Mrs Hutchinson.

Ralph and his wife saw Mrs Hutchinson several times during their time in Checkley Rectory. On one occasion, Mrs

The old rectory at Checkley.

Phillips heard her name being called while she was alone in the house. Then a meeting of the parish council being held in the rectory was interrupted by repeated knocking on the door. The members decided that it must have been the formidable Mrs Hutchinson disapproving of some item on the agenda.

The ghost of the formidable widow does not restrict itself to the house. In 1939 she was seen at the Hutchinson Memorial School by the new headmistress, Miss Hilda Stonehouse. She saw an old lady walking with a stick across the school playground, and assumed it was a visitor coming to see her housekeeper. However, the housekeeper was adamant that she had received no visitors. The following week Miss Stonehouse was visiting the rectory and saw a painting on the wall. She recognised the mysterious visitor, wearing the same grey dress, waistcoat and mobcap. It was, of course, a portrait of Mrs Hutchinson.

Miss Stonehouse used to cut across the churchyard every day to get to the schoolhouse. She was not in the least worried about the tall stories told by the villagers, who avoided the path because of a feeling of being watched there. She knew the path well, and was happily walking along it one evening in the dark, when something impeded her progress. She could not see anyone or any obstruction, but found she could not get any further. She had to retrace her steps back to the church and then walk home via the road.

Hilda loved to play the church organ, and the rector allowed her to do so whenever she wished. When she had finished her playing, she would turn off the lights, feel her way to the door, lock it, then return the key to the rectory. She was never afraid of being alone in the dark church, but on several occasions she saw a hooded figure near the altar. When she told the rector about the figure, he informed her that he had seen it himself, and so had the village postmistress. The figure seemed to be that of a hooded monk, wearing a robe and cowl. It is thought that it might be the ghost of the last abbot of Croxden, Thomas Chawney. When Henry VIII dissolved the monasteries, the abbey passed into the hands of 'a dissolute adventurer' named Geoffrey Foljambe. As the abbot's grave is in the chancel of Checkley church, lying alongside the graves of members of the dissolute Foljambe family, it is thought that he finds their company repugnant. However, everyone who has seen the figure of the monk finds it a friendly presence, and not in the least frightening.

GHOSTS OF UTTOXETER

When Julie Crutchley was six years old, her family moved into the George and Dragon, a public house in Carter Street, Uttoxeter. The building had three floors, the top one being an unused attic. In 1974, the attic was renovated, converted into two bedrooms. Julie moved into the larger of the two.

Shortly after this, she began to see three ghosts. One was a solemn-looking man who looked to be in his mid-thirties. Another was an elderly woman, and the third was a boy. She didn't see them all together very often, but the woman often stood by Julie's bed, smiling at her. The boy was in the habit of sitting on the floor, close to the bed. The man was different, and always kept his distance. He would walk away if Julie looked directly at him.

'It seemed that whenever I woke in the night and looked over my bedcovers,' Julie recalled, 'I saw at least one of them. I was very scared, as you can imagine, and I quickly went back under the covers."

She told her parents about her ghostly visitors, but they dismissed them as inventions of her childish imagination. However, Julie continued to see these visitors until the family left the George and Dragon in 1980. Now an adult, and living in Kent, Julie often looks back on her childhood and she remembers her three ghosts. She states firmly, 'I have to say, with my hand on my heart, that what I saw was not in any way a figment of my imagination.'

The whole story was brought back into Julie's mind when her sister Wendy contacted her from Uttoxeter. The George and Dragon had been converted into bedsit flats, and one of the tenants had asked Wendy whether the place was haunted when it was a pub. Apparently, Julie's ghosts are back!

When Geoff Startin was in his twenties, he was sitting in Uttoxeter Parish church with his friend Alan. Geoff looked up and saw the figure of a grey-haired lady in the balcony. He was very puzzled at this, as he and Alan had just explored the whole building, and knew it to be empty. Moreover, they were now sitting by the church door and knew that no-one had come in while they were sitting there.

As he watched, the figure disappeared. Just as he began to wonder whether he had been confused by a trick of the light, Alan asked him, 'Did you see her too, Geoff?' He went on to describe the figure just as Geoff had seen her.

The two young men went up to the balcony to see if they could find the lady, but there was no-one there. Geoff is now an Anglican clergyman in South Wales, and he told me that he can still remember the ghostly figure with her shock of grey hair.

Geoff also told me about an incident that occurred in Uttoxeter in the late 1970s, when workmen at Bamford's factory in Pinfold Street were terrified by the ghost of a dark-haired woman in black. It was alleged to be the ghost of Emily Bamford who died in the 1880s. Emily was the young wife of Henry Bamford, one of the second generation of the family that founded the famous JCB firm. Emily often used to visit the Pinfold Street premises with her husband, to talk to the factory hands. It is not know why her ghost should continue to haunt the premises, though there is a story that she actually died at the factory during one of her visits.

LUD'S CHURCH

One of the most mysterious and magical places in Staffordshire is situated in the north of the county, north of Leek, north of the magnificent hills of the Roaches, and hidden in Back Forest Wood. Lud's Church – sometimes written as Ludchurch – is not a building at all, but a ravine

200 feet long and 50 feet deep. I went there on Midsummer's Day 2004 with John Kay from Swythamley. Walking through the wood, it would be quite easy to miss the entrance in the rocks, but John pointed it out. We climbed down rough-hewn stone steps, curving down to the right. The central chamber of the ravine is about ten feet in width, though it soon narrows again to about six feet. The climb out at the far end is a steep incline, and comes out onto open moorland.

On the path to Lud's Church, we passed a strange rock formation, known as Hanging Rock. There are many legends associated with this rock, including gruesome tales of human sacrifice.

Hanging Rock.

More mystical tales involve moon worship, and contemporary visitors report seeing a hare that spends much of its time at both Hanging Rock and Lud's Church. The hare has long been associated in folklore with the moon.

The ravine at Lud's Church is steeped in history and legend. Robin Hood, Friar Tuck and Bonny Prince Charlie are all reputed to have hidden from the authorities within the chasm, but its most famous connection is with the story of Sir Gawain and the Green Knight. This tale was written by an unknown poet in the 14th century in an old North Midland dialect, peculiar to North Staffordshire. Dr David Clarke, in his *Guide To Britain's Pagan Heritage*, suggests that the poet may have been a monk at Dieulacres Abbey near Leek. In the tale, Sir Gawain travels up from Camelot following a challenge by the Green Knight, and finally tracks him down in a ravine called the Green Chapel, believed to be Lud's Church.

Another legend of Lud's Church dates from the early 15th century, when the Lollards – supporters of the doctrines of the early Protestant clergyman John Wycliffe – were challenging the established church. One of their main demands was for a bible printed in English that ordinary people could access, but this was regarded as outrageous. The king declared the Lollards heretics and banned their services. They nevertheless continued to meet secretly, and one place that was ideal for the hidden meetings was the isolated ravine at Lud's Church.

The leader of the local Lollards was a 70-year-old man called Walter de Lud Auk. His name has led some to claim that

The entrance down into the ravine called Lud's Church.
© *photo by Lesley Hextall*

Lud's Church was named after him, but according to local writer and newspaper editor Doug Pickford it is more likely that Walter took his name from the place where he held his meetings.

On one tragic Sunday fourteen Lollards were taking part in a service, and among them was Alice de Lud Auk, Walter's 18-year-old granddaughter, who possessed a pure singing voice. Despite the isolation of the spot, the king's soldiers succeeded in tracking down this group of Staffordshire heretics. As the soldiers attempted to arrest the Lollards, young Alice was killed. For many years, high up on a ledge of the ravine, there was a wooden figure of a young woman. It was the figurehead of a sailing ship, the *Swythamley*, and may have been placed in Lud's Church as a tribute to Alice de Lud Auk. A picture of it can be seen in the nearby youth hostel at Gradbach. Another mysterious phenomenon that has been seen there is a silent white owl that glides through the ravine, even in the daytime. Again, many visitors say that it is the spirit of young Alice.

However, Lud's Church was used for worship long before the Lollards, and even before the legend of The Green Knight. This hidden place was used for pagan ceremonies in ancient times. Dr David Clarke, in his *Ghosts and Legends of the Peak District*, writes that 'Lud's Church' may well be a corruption of 'Lug's Church', named after the sun-god. The sun can only shine into the deep ravine on Midsummer's Day, and this would certainly have led to pagan worshipers regarding it as a place of special importance. Doug Pickford and Andy Collins visited Lud's Church at midday on Midsummer's Day 1993, and they were thrilled to find that the sun did indeed penetrate the chasm. In his book, *Earth Mysteries of the Three Shires*, Doug describes how the golden rays of the sun illuminated and warmed the chasm on that day of the summer solstice.

For pagans, Lud's Church retains all its ancient significance and power, present in the chasm for thousands of years. Jackie Barfoot visited Lud's Church at Lammas (1 August) 2002 and found it awe-inspiring. She felt it was a place of death and rebirth, a place of initiation and sacrifice. She says, 'We saw faces and images in the rocks and crevices, and, being empathic, I had a feeling that a young man was once initiated there into the mysteries of the Goddess. Ludchurch comes across as an entrance to the otherworld, and to the womb of mother earth.'

Another follower of the old ways is Sheena McDonagh, who writes, 'Ludchurch is one of those places that seems to appear and disappear at will. After many years of searching, I eventually found Ludchurch, thanks to a friend, Gavin, who had spent a few months near there at a Scout Camp in the 1980s. I was amazed at the depth of the greenery there as I stepped down the slippery steps into the chasm, but my only problem was that I couldn't progress beyond the halfway point. I became rooted to the spot, and couldn't bring myself to move forward. I don't know what I encountered in there that day, but whatever it was wouldn't let me walk through the cleft. I just got a huge sense of foreboding. I wasn't scared, but all the hairs on the back of my neck stood on end. I felt that it was a place of death, had some connection to the dead, maybe an Underworld passage.'

THE GIRL IN BROUGH PARK: Leek

It was a June afternoon, and Roger Turner was in Brough Park, Leek, with what he describes as his 'best inanimate friend': his metal detector. He was on an ancient cobbled path, known as Dickie's Gutter, which runs steeply downhill alongside the Garden of Remembrance. The path is shaded by overhanging trees, and is close to St Edward's Church. It runs by the area known as Petite France, where Napoleonic prisoners of war are buried.

Roger decided to use his metal detector to do a search by the edge of the footpath, as he knew that merry people sauntering home from the local pubs often lose coins from

Dickie's Gutter, Brough Park, Leek.

their pockets. He turned his scanner on and he'd only walked six paces when there was a sudden signal from the metal detector. He knew he'd found something, and was pleased to see it was a coin. He hoped that it might even be an old 'bun head' penny.

When he checked he could hardly believe his luck. It was a genuine silver half-crown from the 1930s. To say he was thrilled and excited would be an understatement. Before cleaning the soil off, he glanced round to see if the park-keeper might be watching. Using a metal detector in the park was not an officially approved hobby.

However, what he saw left him amazed and speechless. Sitting with her back to the sandstone wall was the most fascinating girl he had ever seen. She had a dark complexion, which Roger described to me as 'gypsy-like', and waist-long coiled hair 'as black as a raven's wing'. She was dressed in a black chiffon lace dress with dazzling white collar and cuffs. She was sitting with her knees drawn up, with her fingers interlocked over her knee-length cross-laced boots. Roger told me, 'She was like someone from a Victorian family photograph.'

When Roger tried to explain to her what he was doing with the metal detector, he found he was unable to speak a word. He even dropped the precious coin he'd just found. He turned to pick it up, and felt the temperature plummet from that of a warm June afternoon to that of an icy winter's day. When he turned back to the girl, she had vanished without trace.

Roger is a rational man, ex-RAF, and trained not to panic easily, so he walked over to where the uncanny supernatural apparition had been sitting. The only evidence of her having been there was the faint but unmistakable aroma of rose-scented perfume.

He tells me that he often checks in his find box to make sure that his silver 1933 half-crown is real, as it is the only tangible evidence of the memorable encounter with the beautiful apparition in Brough Park in 1993. He wonders if the coin had once belonged to the mysterious girl.

THE MERMAID'S POOL: Thorncliffe

The pool, officially called Black Mere, is situated in an area known as Morridge, in moorlands three miles north-east from the town of Leek and two miles from the village of Thorncliffe. It is close to the 1603 feet hill called Merryton Low. It has frequently been stated that no animal would drink from the pool and no bird would fly over it, although this strongly held local belief was questioned by the 17th century scientist Dr Robert Plot, who described a visit to the pool in his book, A Natural History of Staffordshire, published in 1686.

Its official name may be Black Mere, but everyone in North Staffordshire knows it as the Mermaid's Pool. This is because the pool's greatest claim to fame is the mermaid that inhabits its depths. She is not a benevolent creature. There is another Mermaid's Pool on Kinder Scout in Derbyshire, who brings good fortune to anyone who manages to see her. The Black Mere mermaid is very different. She entices any passer-by who spots her into the pool, then takes him down to a certain death by drowning.

One tradition alleges that the mermaid was a beautiful young woman who was accused of witchcraft by a rejected suitor, named Joseph Linnett. The practice was that any woman accused of witchcraft would be bound and thrown into a deep pond. If she floated she was guilty of witchcraft and would be taken out of the pool and hanged. If she sank and drowned, then she was innocent of the charge. Innocent but dead! She was not going to survive either way. The Thorncliffe girl was thrown into Black Mere and she drowned, thus proving her innocence.

However, a few weeks later, the body of Joseph Linnett – the cruel man she'd rejected and who had accused her in a petty act of spite – was found floating in the pool with scratches of sharp talons on his face. The legend quickly grew that she had turned into a mermaid and would seize any passing man to drown him.

If you should seek refuge from this gruesome tale by going to the nearby inn, you will find no safe haven. The inn is called The Mermaid, and on the wall you can read the chilling words that if the mermaid "calls on you to greet her, she ups and drags you down."

At the end of the 19th century, workmen were instructed to drain the pool. However the task was never carried out. The men claimed that the mermaid had appeared to them. On

STAFFORDSHIRE
Ghost Stories

this occasion she didn't take the men to their watery death, but she warned them that if the waters of Black Mere escaped the confines of the pool, the whole of Leek would be submerged in water and all would drown. The town of Leek is still there and the pool is still there, so obviously the workmen took the mermaid's threat seriously.

THE HIGHLAND DRUMMER BOY: Tompkin

The small hamlet of Tompkin lies about two miles south-east of Endon, and it owes its name to a macabre and horrific event in the 1740s. The supporters of Bonny Prince Charlie had come south from Scotland to try to recover the English throne for the Stuarts. There were numerous groups of Highland soldiers passing through Staffordshire and Derbyshire. They were living off the land, and would often turn up at a house and billet themselves there for a few days.

One place they occupied was the hall belonging to Squire Murhall, a brutal and cruel man. He was used to getting his own way, and was very resentful of these Scottish soldiers who were sleeping at his home, eating his food and drinking his wine. Full of resentment, he seethed with rage, but could do nothing as the visitors – about fifteen of them – were armed and not at all impressed at the bluster of the pompous squire.

After a week or so, they moved on, heading for Derby. Once they had departed, Squire Murhall regained his lost courage and, together with a male servant, he decided to follow the Highlanders at a safe distance. He was delighted when he

came across a Scottish drummer boy named Tam, who had been unable to keep up with his comrades. He seized the boy, and hauled him back to the hall. He decided to make an example of the 15-year-old, to show people that it wasn't a good idea to cross the squire. He had the boy slain and then skinned. He compounded this heinous crime by using the boy's skin to make a drum. He even had the drum hung in Endon church, adding blasphemy to his other sins.

In the days that followed, whenever anything went awry in the Endon area – cattle dying, men having accidents, children becoming ill – the local people would mutter that it was because of the drum made of human skin hanging in the church. Eventually they took the drum down and removed the skin, which they buried in the unmarked grave of the boy Tam.

Squire Murhall did not escape scot free. The Highland soldiers came back looking for Tam, and when they heard that the squire had murdered him, they gave the man a beating so severe that it left him crippled for the rest of his life, and it is impossible to feel any shred of sympathy for him.

The whole story is horrific and brutal, but one fact is of interest to anyone interested in the origins of place names. The spot where the evil act had taken place was known as Tam's Skin, which later transformed into Tamskin, then Tomskin. Today it is known as Tompkin.

RED STOCKINGS : Wetwood

The ghost of a young Cavalier known as Red Stockings haunts Broughton Hall, which is situated half a mile from the village of Wetwood, on the road from Eccleshall to Loggerheads. The ghost's nickname is explained by the manner in which he died. During the English Civil War, the Broughton family were staunch royalists. When the young heir to the estate saw a troop of Parliamentary soldiers marching up the Hall drive, he threw open an upstairs window and called out, 'I am for the king!'

This proved both brave and foolhardy, because the Cromwellian soldiers immediately opened fire at him, and he was struck in the chest. As he staggered down the Long Gallery, the blood from his wounds flowed down and soaked his stockings, turning them deep red. The wound proved fatal and he died minutes later. The blood also stained the floorboards, and these stains remained visible until the floor was replaced in the 1920s.

Since that fateful day, the ghost of Red Stockings has been seen many times, always in the Long Gallery. In 1880, members of the Yonge family were visiting Broughton Hall. The children of the two families were playing hide and seek and one of the visitors, an eleven-year-old girl, hid in the Long Gallery. She peeped out from her hiding place and saw Red Stockings gazing out of the window. Assuming it was one of the Broughton boys, she crept past him and ran downstairs. At the foot of the stairs she saw the boy she thought she'd seen upstairs and asked him how he'd got down so quickly without being seen. Lady Broughton heard

Broughton Hall, Wetwood
© Bruce Braithwaite

the girl, and she later told the girl's parents that the child had definitely seen the resident ghost, Red Stockings.

On another occasion in the early 1900s, guests were attending a formal party at Broughton Hall. One lady apologised to her hosts, saying that she hadn't realised it was a fancy dress party until she'd seen a young man in Cavalier costume. 'Was he in red stockings?' she was asked. 'Yes,' she replied, 'and he was looking out of the Long Gallery window.' Another sighting of the resident ghost.

A year or two later, a cleaner was scrubbing the stairs that led to the Long Gallery. When she saw a young man in red stockings approaching, she moved her bucket to let him pass. To her horror, the figure passed clean through her. After this experience, she refused to clean the stairs again unless she had someone with her.

Sir Delves Broughton sold the hall in 1914, and it was occupied until the 1990s by Franciscan nuns, who continued to say regular prayers for the young man known as Red Stockings.

The Yonge family mentioned above were from nearby Charnes Manor, a house that has its own ghost. One evening in the late 1600s, a young woman appeared in the drawing room. She was dressed in a shroud, and she was bleeding profusely from the stump of a severed finger. She was recognised immediately as the young wife of the owner, who had died and been placed in the family vault that very day. But amazingly she was not a ghost. She had been in a coma and only thought to be dead. An avaricious coachman had noted that she had been placed in the vault still wearing an expensive gold wedding ring. Deciding that he would steal it, he crept into the vault and cut off the ring finger with a sharp knife. When the corpse bled and then sat up, the coachman fled the scene. It did him no good, as he was tracked down and hanged, although the ring was never recovered.

The lady who had been thought dead lived on for many years. However, the fingerless figure of a lady in a shroud has been seen many times since, and now it really is her ghost, still searching for her gold ring.

MOLLY LEIGH: Burslem

If you had lived in Burslem in 1700, you would have been very wary of young Molly Leigh. Although she was only 15, she was said to be a strong-willed and difficult girl. If she stared at you with her wild eyes, she could cause you to become ill. If you annoyed her, your cattle would probably become lame. She never went to church, and in those days that was thought to be an indication that she might well be a witch.

Margaret Leigh – always known as Molly – lived in an isolated cottage at Jackfield, on the edge of the moorland, and she made a living by selling milk from her small herd of cows to passers-by. Her enemies used to mutter that she watered down the milk before selling it, but no one would dare say it to her face. She had no friends, and preferred her own company to that of her neighbours.

Her only companion was her pet raven, which perched on her shoulder as she walked about the village. Everyone said that the bird was her familiar, her contact with the devil. When Molly was in her cottage, the raven was in the habit of sitting on the roof watching who walked past. People were convinced that the bird used to tell Molly exactly who had passed by.

One person who loathed Molly with a fierce intensity was the local vicar, the Revd Thomas Spencer. He came to believe that when he saw the bird perched on the inn-sign of the Turk's Head, it would report back to Molly on how frequently he was in there. Moreover, if he shouted abuse at the bird, it would frequently turn his beer sour. One morning, the parson was foolish enough to fire a shot at the raven but he missed. For the next three weeks, the man found himself in terrible agony and unable to walk. In the eyes of the local people, there was an obvious connection between the two events.

Unlike the vicar, some local residents regarded her with respect and awe. She was a witch, that was obvious, but she was their own Burslem witch. If you left her alone, she would do you no harm. A few villagers, less superstitious than the rest, even said that she was just a lonely old woman, not a witch at all.

Molly lived to the age of 63, and died suddenly in March 1748. On 1 April, Spencer had her buried in St John's churchyard. Because she was a witch, he had her buried in a grave that lay north–south instead of the conventional east–west.

The grave of Molly Leigh in St John's Churchyard, Burslem.

After Molly's funeral the vicar and his cronies went to the Turk's Head. After drinking several tankards of hot punch to fortify themselves, they set off across Jackfield to 'purify' Molly's home by means of prayers and hymn-singing. When they got to the cottage, the mourners hung back in trepidation, and indicated that Revd Thomas Spencer should go in first on his own.

He hesitated for a moment, then flung open the door and marched in. Seconds later, he raced out again and headed swiftly back to the Turk's Head, followed by the curious villagers. After yet another drink, the parson solemnly informed them that when he'd entered the cottage, he'd seen Molly Leigh – or her ghost – sitting by her hearth.

As Molly was obviously too much for just one priest, Spencer enlisted the help of three more – the neighbouring vicars of Newchapel, Stoke and Wolstanton. At midnight on the following Sunday, the four clergymen approached Molly's grave, chanting prayers. They ordered the sexton to disinter her coffin and to open the lid. As the four nervous parsons peered into the coffin, they were startled by a loud croaking sound. They looked up and saw that it was Molly's raven, perched on the tomb and gazing at them. The cruel Parson Spencer grabbed the fluttering bird and threw it into the coffin. He slammed the lid shut, trapping the still living bird in the coffin with the body of Molly Leigh. They later piled extra stones on top of the tomb, to keep the spirit of Molly and her raven from escaping.

Later the four brave vicars summoned enough courage to return to Molly's cottage, where they prayed that Molly's ghost should leave the locality for evermore. Their prayer was not successful as the ghost of Molly Leigh has been seen throughout the centuries ever since her death in 1748. Some say that her ghost can be heard singing 'Weight and measure sold I never, Milk and water sold I ever,' an obvious reference to her alleged practice of selling watered-down milk during her lifetime.

Even as late as the 20th century, Burslem coal miners would not go down the pit if they met a cross-eyed woman on their way to work. They thought that it might be Molly, the Burslem witch, giving them the evil eye. Alf Booth of Hanley tells me that her ghost is still seen in St John's churchyard, and has often been seen by his friend, whose bedroom overlooks the cemetery.

One elderly lady tells me that, as a girl, she and her friends would skip round Molly's grave chanting, 'Molly Leigh, Molly Leigh, Chase me round the apple tree.' They then used to flee for their lives, convinced that they had caused her ghost to come back.

GHOST IN A POLICE HOSTEL: Baswich

Ray Fallows, a police cadet with the Staffordshire Police Force, was based in a cadet hostel in the grounds of Baswich House, near Stafford. The hostel was in an old building that had once been servants' quarters.

In November 1968, Ray and his fellow cadets had been out in the Peak District, taking part in an Outward Bound course. When they got to Stafford late on the Sunday evening, most of the other cadets went back to their parents'

Baswich House, demolished in 2013.
© *Illustration by Julie Rebecca Saunt*

houses for the night, but Ray didn't. Because he was due to start work early the next day, he decided he'd stay in the hostel. The building was locked, but Ray managed to ease a window open to gain access. He wasn't in the least concerned about being on his own in the empty building. He made his way to his room and went to bed.

As he lay there, he was surprised to hear the sound of footsteps on the upstairs landing. He was absolutely sure that he was the only person in the building. The footsteps were slow and unhurried. He tried to put the sounds out of his mind, but couldn't. He was somewhat relieved when, after some minutes, the sounds ceased. However, he now had a sensation that someone had entered the room. He had left the curtains open, and moonlight was shining in. This light was enough to tell him that he could see no one there. But then, to the cadet's horror, he felt the weight of someone sitting down on his bed.

He lay still for a minute or so, then, summoning his courage, he sat bolt upright. The weight disappeared from his bed, and the strange feelings disappeared. Ray admits that he did not get much sleep that night.

On Monday morning, all the other cadets came back, and Ray told his room-mate, Dave Smith, about his weird overnight experience. Dave, of course, thought it was hilarious. 'Dave just fell about laughing,' Ray told me. Ray had to endure a couple of weeks of Dave taking the mickey out of him, but then the roles were reversed. Dave Smith had to spend a Sunday night in the hostel on his own, and he changed his attitude completely. 'You know that story you told me,' he said. 'Well, I certainly believe you now! Last night the same thing happened to me. I heard the footsteps upstairs and I felt someone come in and sit on my bed.'

The two cadets decided that they would not tell any of their other colleagues about their ghostly experiences as they knew they would become the target of much banter and derision. They did, however, make some enquiries about the history of the building. They heard that a manservant had hanged himself there, after falling in love with one of the maids. Although the girl returned his affections, their employer had disapproved of their romance and had forbidden them from seeing each other. The girl was sent away from Baswich House, and the distraught young man killed himself.

Ray and Dave wondered whether their ghostly visitor might be the hanged servant, still forlornly searching for his forbidden sweetheart.

MYSTERIES OF THE SHEPHERD'S MONUMENT:
Shugborough

Shugborough Hall is situated in the centre of Staffordshire, and was the home of the Fifth Earl of Lichfield, better known as the photographer Patrick Lichfield. It is part of a historic estate, with a working farm, dairy, watermill, brewhouse and kitchens, and it is visited by a quarter of a million people every year.

The hall has a number of resident ghosts including Admiral George Anson (1697–1762), an ancestor of Lord Lichfield, Lady Harriet, who died in childbirth in the State Bedroom, and a former housekeeper who is also said to haunt the kitchens. In the 1980s, after the last of the tourists had gone, decorator John Smith was painting in the Great Hall. He was interrupted by a knocking on the door, but could find no one there. This was repeated several times a day over the next week. When he mentioned it to the staff they said it was the ghost of Admiral Anson, but John was sure it was a light feminine knock and thinks it was more likely to have been Lady Harriet.

However, the most mysterious object at Shugborough is not in the hall itself but in the grounds. This is the Shepherd's Monument, which has a marble relief of shepherds and shepherdesses.

Commissioned by Admiral Anson in 1748, it was carved by a Dutch sculptor but was based on a painting, *Les Bergers d'Arcadie*, by Nicolas Poussin. Poussin was a Grand Master of the Knights Templar and both the painting and the monument have always been the subject of speculation. Its

44

The shepherd's Monument at Shugborough Hall.
©Lesley Hextall

layout has been connected with the secrets of the Knights Templar, traditionally the keepers of the secrets of the Holy Grail. The legends of the Holy Grail, or Sangreal, have fascinated scholars for centuries, and have connections with both Christian and Celtic myths. The Holy Grail is the vessel from which Jesus drank at the Last Supper. Joseph of Arimathea is said to have brought the vessel to England.

At some time it disappeared, and thousands of searchers have been trying to discover its whereabouts ever since. Some claim that the monument points to the location of the Holy Grail being in England, in Turkey, or even in Nova Scotia. There is that reference to Arcadia, the old name for Nova Scotia, and Admiral Thomas Anson did visit there himself.

As well as the carving of the shepherds, the monument has a series of letters on it in the following pattern:

O U O S V A V V
D   M

© Lesley Hextall

These have puzzled scholars for centuries. Among eminent visitors who have tried to decipher their meaning are Charles Darwin and Josiah Wedgwood. Professional codebreakers have suggested that, to understand what the Shepherd's Monument might mean, it is necessary to take into account not only the letters, but also the image of the shepherds, and the geometry of the shepherds' hands and staffs.

However, it has to be said that there are as many theories as there are researchers. As well as those seeking clues to the location of the Holy Grail, the Shepherd's Monument at Shugborough has been claimed by Ufologists, students of Nostradamus, Jacobite sympathisers, numerologists, alchemists and believers in the ways of Wicca (Shugborough actually means place of the witch). Then there are others who claim that it is simply a secret message between lovers.

The mysteries remain. Richard Kemp, the estate manager at Shugborough, says, 'It's like Everest; you climb it because it's there. There's a code here, so everyone wants to unravel it.'

THE BLOODY STEPS: Rugeley

The ghost seen by two women in 1939 was a blood-curdling sight. It was a summer evening and they were by the Trent and Mersey Canal in Rugeley at a spot known as the Bloody Steps, close to Brindley's Bank. When they heard a wailing cry, they looked up and there he was. His feet were shrouded in a foggy vapour but the rest of him was clearly visible.

He had long black hair and doleful expression on his face. His clothes were black and white, and he was wearing knickerbockers. As they watched, he glided across the grass in front of them and disappeared through the railings of the Waterworks.

The name of the Bloody Steps dates back to 1839, and derives from the brutal murder of Christina Collins. She was a young married woman who was travelling from Liverpool to London to join her husband, Robert, who had found a job as an ostler there. She was travelling on a Pickford & Co. boat on the Trent and Mersey canal – a cheaper way of travel than by stagecoach – but she was molested and then murdered by the drunken crew, James Owen, George Thomas and William Ellis. They then threw Christina's body into the canal, where it was discovered the next day, 17 June. Her body was carried up the steps in Rugeley, and it was said that her blood stained the steps, and afterwards they were always called 'the Bloody Steps'.

The boat's crew were arrested in Fazeley, and the three men were charged with murder. A fourth member of the crew, a boy named William Musson, was exonerated. Two of the

The Bloody Steps.

men, Owen and Thomas, were publicly hanged for their crime in front of a crowd of ten thousand spectators in Stafford, and the third, Ellis, was transported to Australia.

Christina's body was buried in St Augustine's churchyard in Rugeley, and the tragic story of her death is recorded on her tombstone.

'To the memory of Christina Collins, Wife of Robert Collins, London, who, having been barbarously treated was found dead in the Canal in this parish on June 17th 1839 Aged 37 years. This Stone is erected by some individuals of the Parish of Rugeley in Commiseration of the End of the Unhappy Woman'.

It was to this grave that the two women who had seen the ghost made their way in June 1939. Their feeling of awe and ill-ease was increased when they read the words, and realised that it was the exact hundredth anniversary of the murder of poor Christina Collins.

But who was the ghost? It was male and so it was definitely not that of the murdered woman. They thought that it was probably that of the bereaved Robert Collins. The young couple were known to be deeply in love, and it was Robert's name that Christina called out as she died. It seems likely that the ghost of Robert Collins still haunts the scene of his wife's untimely death.

Crime writer Colin Dexter used the plot of the Christina Collins murder case in an Inspector Morse story, which he entitled *The Wench is Dead*, though he did change the outcome. He even moved the action from Rugeley to Oxford.

The grave of Christina Collins in St Augustine's churchyard, Rugeley.

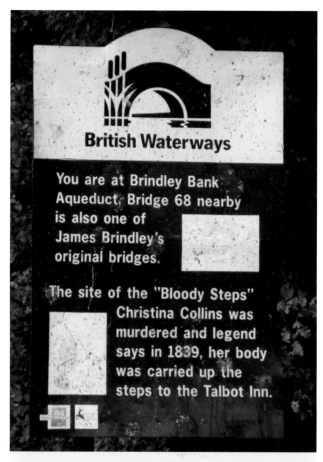

Notice by the side of the Trent and Mersey canal in Rugeley,
opposite the Bloody Steps.

THE SKELETON TREE: Hednesford

Mary Sherwood of Hednesford was in love with her young man, Richard Gordon, but he did have one bad fault. Personally, I think that if a girl has found a man with only one bad fault, she is on to a winner! Richard's fault – his weakness – was his love of poaching. Of course he enjoyed the meat from the animals he caught, but the truth was that he also enjoyed pitting his wits against the rangers and gamekeepers who were out to catch him.

Mary and Richard did all their courting out on Cannock Chase, under their special oak tree. It was there that she persuaded him to promise to give up poaching once they were married. She was a pretty girl and very determined. Richard was so in love that eventually he agreed, and a date was set for the marriage.

The night before the wedding, Richard and his friends went out on what today we would call a pub crawl. His friends were all laughing at the way that Mary had got him to give up his pastime, and accusing him of being already under her thumb. They had visited several taverns, and were somewhat the worse for drink, when one friend had a brilliant idea. Since the No More Poaching vow didn't begin until the next day, the day of the wedding, the men could have one last night of fun on Cannock Chase.

None of the merry group was in any condition to move about quietly. As they stood under the oak tree loudly discussing the poaching they would do, a gamekeeper heard them. He stepped out from the trees and challenged the poachers. One of Richard's cronies pulled out a gun and a shot rang out. The keeper fell to the ground, fatally wounded.

The Skeleton Tree.
© Illustration by Julie Rebecca Saunt

Everyone except Richard ran away. When the other keepers arrived on the scene, it was Richard Gordon – the well-known local poacher – who was found kneeling by the dying man. He was arrested and tried for murder. He was found guilty and sentenced to be hanged.

Of course, Mary was distraught with grief. In the days leading up to Richard's hanging, she took to wandering about on the Chase, singing and weeping and talking to herself, she had been driven half mad with grief. She never went home at night, but slept in the open, under the tree that had been so special to her and Richard. On the day that her lover was hanged, Mary Sherwood drowned herself in the lake. The two young lovers lost their lives at the same hour on the same day. On that day, all the leaves fell from their special oak tree, and it has never borne any new leaves to this day.

Everyone in the locality calls it 'the skeleton tree'. It is still there, leafless, to this day. And the ghosts of Mary and Richard are seen on summer nights, sitting together under the skeleton tree.

THE HORN DANCE: Abbots Bromley

When 27-year-old Jacky Ayre visited Abbotts Bromley with her parents in 1988, she had a very strange experience. Her father was keen to see the ancient reindeer horns which hang in the church. These are the horns of native British reindeer

The reindeer horns in Abbots Bromley church.

and have been carbon dated to 1065.

Her parents immediately made their way over to where the horns were hanging, but Jacky found herself transfixed. 'I couldn't move without great effort,' she told me, 'and I felt strange and uneasy.' As the feeling grew into intense discomfort, she forced herself to walk out. 'It was like trying to wade through treacle,' she recalled. Once outside, she felt better. Walking round the outside of the building, she encountered a pocket of very cold air. Although it was in direct June sunshine, the spot was almost freezing. Jacky realised that she was outside the part of the church where the reindeer horns were hanging inside.

A few years later, Jacky and her parents went back to Abbotts Bromley on Wakes Monday – early in September – to watch the famous horn dance. Jacky returned to the church to see what would happen. The horns were not there, of course, as they were being carried by the horn dancers. This time she was able to move without difficulty, but she still had the same uneasy sensation and had to leave the church.

The annual horn dance takes place on 'the Monday following the first Sunday after 4th September', and it a very ancient rite. Dr Robert Plot wrote about it in 1686, but the nature of the dance suggests that it goes back much further. In Dr Plot's time, the dance took place in mid-winter, rather than in early September.

There are six sets of horns, each mounted on wooden deer-heads, three of which are painted white and three black. Six men carry the horns, but other performers in the dancing include a fool in jester's motley, a bowman, a hobbyhorse, a boy known as Robin Hood, and a large farmer dressed in women's clothing and known as Maid Marian. There is also a musician. When I watched the dance in 2008, the musician was an accordionist, but in earlier years there was a violin, and before that a pipe and drum.

The dance begins with a silent single file of dancers who form a figure of eight, but when the music starts, the horn bearers face each other. Three times they advance as if to lock horns and twice they retreat. On the third advance they pass through, one set of bearers carrying the horn high and the others low. Today the dancers are the main participants of the event, but Dr Plot described the event as a hobbyhorse dance, and then mentioned the horn bearers as an afterthought.

The early Christians were not at all keen on this ancient pagan ritual, and in the seventh century the Archbishop of Canterbury banned 'the devilish putting on the head or horns of beasts'. The church today is a bit more tolerant, but the horns are kept in the church when they are not being used, in order to tame their pagan power.

On Wakes Monday, after a 7am service, the horns are taken out of the church, and the first dance is performed for the vicar. I was amused to discover that the jester and the cross-dressing Maid Marian are omitted from this performance. Perhaps they are too bawdy and irreverent for the church. The next three dances take place in Abbots Bromley itself, then the performers set out on a twenty-mile tour of the area, dancing at farms, Blithfield Hall – home of Lady

The Abbots Bromley horn dance in 2004.

Bagot, outside humble cottages and even on the lawn of a modern bungalow overlooking the nearby reservoir. The final evening dance takes back in Abbots Bromley. The horns are then returned to their place in St Nicholas's Church, and the dancers go off to the pub for a drink. Considering the dancers are given a pint at each place where they perform – I did see a few opt for a soft drink – a night's drinking and revelry may leave a few the worse for wear. Or perhaps the drinking and revelry are what the true spirit of the occasion is all about.

By tradition the dancers came from two families, the Fowells and the Bentleys, although today that is relaxed. However, I did find that, in 2004, three generations of Fowells were taking part: the accordionist, one of the dancers and a young Robin Hood.

There is a history of antagonism between the church and the dancers. In 1939, Marcia Alice Rice, the headmistress of the local girls' school, wrote, 'The villagers are at once roused to anger if any vicar ventures to act regarding the horns without the consent of the dancers.' She quoted an example from the late 19th century when the vicar refused to let the dancers take the horns out of the church for a dance. A village meeting was held, and eventually the churchwardens gave their permission. In 1981, the local parish council formally took over the ownership of the horns, although they do still hang in church.

There is dispute whether the dance itself is of Christian or pagan origin. Jackie Barfoot visited the event, and commented, 'To me it invoked the spirit of the horned god, the symbolism of the waning year and the coming season of the rut and the hunt. I thought of it as a blessing to make the forthcoming hunting season fruitful, and also a symbol of a fertility dance imbuing the harvest and orchards with the spirit of the life force of the God and Goddess.'

Marcia Rice did not agree with Dr Plot, who described the event as a sport. 'It is not now, and it never has been, a sport or any kind of amusement,' she wrote. 'Whether deriving from pagan or Christian days, it is and always has been a rite. It creates a sense of wonder and respect.'

THE LAUGHING CAVALIER AND ENTOMBED ELSPETH: Lichfield.

In Bird Street in Lichfield there is an old inn, The King's Head, which has a number of ghosts. One which appears in the function room is that of a young girl who is said to have perished in a fire on the premises. Another is the ghost of a former landlord called George, who appears in the cellar where he died. However, the King's Head's most well-known apparition is the spectre of what is popularly known as the Laughing Cavalier. This is the ghost of a royalist soldier who challenged a parliamentarian roundhead soldier outside the tavern. The cavalier was hacked to death in the ensuing fight, and his ghost is often seen in the King's Head and in the street outside. Although he still bears the wounds inflicted on him, he is permanently cheerful and laughing as he glides through the modern passing traffic and the passers-by.

The King's Head, Bird Street Litchfield

Also in Bird Street there was a furniture shop, where the ghostly figure of a girl of about thirteen was seen on at least two occasions. In 1986, a carpet fitter fled in terror after catching sight of the girl in what he knew was an empty shop. He later said that the girl appeared to be staring at him. The shop owner, Roger Emsley, commented that his carpet fitter was a sensible and down-to-earth man, and certainly not a chap to be easily scared. Nevertheless, the man refused to be alone in the shop ever again.

In that same shop, a cleaner, Ann, was vacuuming an upstairs showroom in 1991, when she became aware that the temperature was plummeting. She turned around and saw an icy vapour forming behind a chair. The mist formed itself into the upper part of a young girl of about thirteen. She was wearing a shawl and a bonnet. Her wispy hair appeared to be a pale ginger colour, and her thin face was pinched and dirty. Ann felt that the girl's sad expression made her want to cry. Ann recalled that although the girl's mouth didn't move, she could hear a child's voice in her head. It told her that the girl's name was Elspeth, and that the showroom they were in had been the girl's own room.

Just round the corner, in Sandford Street, the owner of a pet shop had become accustomed to the sudden drops in temperature, to the inexplicable movement of stock while his shop was unoccupied, and to the strange, moving shadows that he and his son had both seen. But after the day when he had been reorganising his cellar, there was an increase in odd phenomena. That day, his two dogs came howling and yelping up the cellar steps in a state of panic. The shop owner, Christopher Whitehouse, stated that until that time, the dogs had been quite happy to sleep contentedly in the cellar, but from that day onwards they refused to ever go down again.

In the shop cellar, there is the walled-up entrance to a tunnel which is believed to have formerly led to the vaults of Lichfield Cathedral. There is a local legend that a young girl had been exploring the tunnel, before lying down and falling asleep. While still sleeping, the poor girl was accidentally entombed when the entrance to the subterranean tunnel was sealed up. The ghost seen by both the carpet fitter and by Ann is widely believed to be that of the 13-year-old girl, who died a lonely death, trapped beneath the streets of Lichfield.

Ann was horrified to think that the girl's body may still lie beneath the streets of the town. She says that she herself knew nothing of the legend about the girl, and she had not been told about the frightening experience of the carpet fitter which had occurred five years before she encountered Elspeth.

A LAST VISIT FROM A FRIEND: Elford

The Old Rectory, Elford.

The Revd Francis Paget was the rector of Elford, near Tamworth. In a letter written in 1877, he described a bizarre event that had happened to him a few years earlier.

He was walking along a passage in the rectory one winter afternoon. As he approached the living room, he was surprised to see that the door was shrouded in mist. The spot was usually well lit, as there was a large south-facing window. It was slightly foggy outside, but the mist inside appeared much denser. Francis described the mist as being like a jet of steam exposed to cold air.

As the rector approached, the mist gathered into one spot and intensified, transforming into a human figure. He could see the head and shoulders clearly, while the lower half seemed to be clothed in a long cloak. Where the cloak reached the stone floor it formed a wide circle, and the figure was shaped like a tall pyramid.

Francis Paget later described the figure he saw as 'a statue carved in mist'. Its upper half appeared quite opaque, though the lower part was so transparent he could see the panels of the door through it. At this stage he did not regard the figure as anything supernatural or ghostly, but as a magnificent natural phenomenon caused by the light from the window.

As he stood motionless before the apparition, the head of the figure turned to look at him. The rector immediately recognised the face as that of a dear friend. The expression on the face was kind and peaceful, and not in the least frightening. The mist statue gazed at Francis with a look of kind affection, then the whole thing disappeared. The passageway was empty of any trace of mist.

The rector was awestruck and amazed at what he'd seen, but had no sense of anything fearful. He calmly walked through the spot where the figure had appeared, opened the door and went through into the room where his meal had been set.

The next day, he received news that his friend had died peacefully at the very time he'd seen the mist. He'd had no idea that his friend was ill, let alone that he was dying. He had not been thinking about the friend when he saw the phenomenon, so he could not have conjured up the figure in his imagination.

The Revd Francis Paget decided that his friend had come to him of his own volition to say a final farewell. In his letter, he stated that since that afternoon, every time he walked along the passageway, he remembered his friend with a feeling of awe and with great affection.

Francis's son became the village squire and lived in Elford Hall, next door to the Rectory. The Hall was demolished in 1966, but the rectory where Francis saw the statue made of mist is still there, though now a private residence.

THE GHOST THAT ONLY CHILDREN CAN SEE:
Hopwas

The village of Hopwas has two graveyards: one is attached to St Chad's church on Hopwas Hill, which dates from 1881. There is a much older one in Hints Road where there was once a mission church of St John. It is this latter churchyard that is reputed to be haunted by the ghost of a young boy.

The graveyard in Hints Road, Hopwas.

Twenty years ago, the members of Hopwas WI conducted a survey of the headstones in the two graveyards, registering their positions and dates. They made careful records of the inscriptions on all the gravestones, and this involved taking rubbings of the words. They were extremely careful not to disturb the graves, but in the Hints Road site they did have to pull aside weeds and ivy that were growing over the graves. One of the graves was that of a six-year-old boy, who had died in March 1878.

Later that same week, one of the members, Pat Waugh, was walking past the churchyard with her three-year-old son, Neil, in a pushchair. As they passed the gateway, Neil looked into the graveyard and said, 'Mummy, look, a little boy over there.' Pat couldn't see anything, but Neil repeated, 'Little boy there,' and pointed to the left-hand corner of the churchyard. Pat still couldn't see anyone, so she dismissed it from her mind.

However, the next day she was talking with her friend and fellow WI member, Glen Smith. During the conversation, Glen told Pat about a strange thing that had happened the previous evening. She had been sitting in the lounge with her three-year-old daughter Becky. The girl looked up from what she was doing and exclaimed, 'Mummy, there's a little boy at the window.' Glen looked up and could see nothing, but Becky insisted that a boy was looking in. Glen's house is on Hints Road, about twenty yards from the graveyard, and her lounge window looks out onto the narrow pavement.

When Pat heard Glen's account she felt slightly uneasy, and began to recount what had happened with young Neil claiming he'd seen a little boy in the churchyard. When Pat and Glen told their story to the other WI ladies, they began to wonder if they had disturbed the grave and headstone in any way during the survey. When WI member Rosemary Vanstone told me about the events, she did point out that it was springtime when the child had died, and it was springtime when the gravestone survey was undertaken. The WI ladies also noted that other members of the dead boy's family were not buried in the same churchyard, St John's, but in the newer St Chad's churchyard up on Hopwas Hill. Could it be that he was seeking for the rest of his family?

Of course, it is only youngsters who have seen the boy's ghost, so it might be easy to dismiss the whole thing as children's fantasy. On the other hand, it is well known that children and animals can sometimes sense things that adults have learnt to filter out. And it may be significant that young Neil and Becky had told their parents that they could see the boy on the same day and in the same location, quite independently of each other.

GHOSTS OF TAMWORTH CASTLE

Tamworth was one of the capitals of Mercia, and its castle is over a thousand years old. The first castle was built in 913 by Queen Ethelfleda, but the present castle was constructed in its place by the Norman invaders in 1070.

Tamworth castle.
© Shutterstock/Arena Photo UK

One of its ghosts is that of the Black Lady. She was a Benedictine nun from nearby Polesworth Abbey. Roger de Marmion of Tamworth Castle had seized the Abbey and expelled the nuns, but it was a later Lord Marmion – said to be a wicked and licentious man – who first encountered the ghost. It appeared to him in 1139 and warned him that he would die a painful death unless he gave the abbey back to the nuns. After this threat, the Black Lady struck him a blow with her staff. The wound on his side caused by this blow never healed, and eventually he decided to obey the wishes of his supernatural visitor. He restored the abbey to the nuns, and the wound in his side healed, though he only lived for another four years. Some believe that the nun who appeared in ghostly form was that of St Editha.

The castle also has a White Lady, who appears on the battlements. This lady was the mistress of a knight named Sir Tarquin. As she watched her lover take part in a tournament below, she saw him killed in combat by another knight. At night, the ghost of the White Lady still walks the battlements, weeping silent tears for the death of her lover.

Many other ghosts have been encountered by visitors to the castle and the staff who work there. After a security system was installed, the camera picked up a white 'shadow' in the Great Hall. As Barbara Adams watched the picture, the shape floated across the hall, then suddenly shot off in a different direction. Barbara and a colleague went immediately to the Great Hall to investigate. They could see nothing unusual there, but they both experienced an abnormal chill. An engineer checked the camera and reported that it had no faults and was working properly.

Valerie Lee went to lock a door in the tower one evening. She was on the stairs when the outside door slammed to. When she tried to open it, she found it was locked. The door was normally fastened open with a massive hook. As she knew there was no one else around who could have unfastened the heavy hook, then closed and locked the door, she started to panic. Luckily she was able to radio for a colleague to come and release her from the dark tower.

Another attendant, David Nickels, says that on one occasion he was running up the staircase, and he felt someone running with him, and he is sure that there are supernatural presences there.

On one occasion, Barbara Adams was with the senior attendant and they went into what is now the shop but was then a storeroom. Both of them immediately experienced a terrible pressure, as if something they could not see was crushing them. She admits that it was a frightening experience. However, when she feels the temperature drop – an experience shared by many visitors and staff – she talks to the ghost, telling it that although she can feel its presence, she is not frightened of it.

Sinai House, Shobnall.

SINAI HOUSE: Shobnall

Sinai House is a half-timbered and moated building standing on high ground at Shobnall, near Burton-on-Trent. Originally it was a fortified manor of the de Schobenhale family, but in the early 15th century it was owned by Burton Abbey and used by the monks to meet relatives, or to recover from illnesses or from too much bloodletting. The word Sinai does not come from the bible as I had thought, but from 'soignée', which meant bloodletting in the old French spoken by the Normans. Three times a year, monks from Burton Abbey could visit Sinai House to rest, and to enjoy the delights of Sinai Park, which included deer hunting. The monks built two houses on the site of the previous manor house for their use.

In the reign of Henry VIII, as part of his dissolution of the monasteries, it was taken from the Abbey and given to Sir William Paget, who used it as a hunting lodge. In 1605, the Paget family built a central section joining the two houses, which formed the two wings of the current building.

In 1905 Sinai House was sold on as part of a settlement of a family debt. At one time, the house was used to accommodate RAF personnel. When the house was condemned as unfit for human habitation, it provided shelter for pigs, sheep and hens. Today, the house has been restored and turned into a number of private residences.

Sinai House has numerous ghosts and was featured on the television programme *Most Haunted* in 2005. A phantom horse-drawn coach has been heard by previous tenants of the house, pulling up the driveway, and recently a car on the drive pulled over to let a horse and cart come past, only to find that it had disappeared.

Other ghosts in the house include a hanged witch, and a hooded monk who appears at the foot of the bed in the first-floor bedroom. A ghostly group of Cromwellian soldiers, together with a pack of black dogs, are said to gather round the fire in the front room. One ghost seen in the dining room is that of Sir Henry Paget, who was Wellington's second in command at the battle of Waterloo.

There is also a Grey Lady seen on the bridge over the moat, who is said to be searching for her lost love. This may be the ghost of Isobelle Baker, a local farmer's daughter who worked as a maid at Sinai House at the time the monks stayed there. One of the monks obviously took the phrase about 'enjoyment of the delights of Sinai Park' in the wrong way. He befriended the girl, and then seduced her. She became pregnant, but when she told her secret to her lover, the wicked monk realised that he would be found out. He murdered the pregnant girl, and then, after nightfall, he carried her body to a spot in the grounds where he secretly buried her underneath a tree.

Over the years the tree metamorphosed into the shape of a monk carrying the dead girl. It was therefore always known as the Grey Lady Tree. In the 1990s I accompanied a local man, Nigel Slater, who told me that his childhood playground had been Sinai House and its surrounding fields.

He was keen that I should see the Grey Lady Tree for myself, but when we got to the spot, the tree had gone. It had been completely rooted out and removed. All that was left was a circular depression in the earth. To say that Nigel was outraged would be an understatement. He was very angry indeed, saying that whoever had uprooted it had taken away part of his childhood and, more importantly, a vital element of the local heritage. However, he was able to show me a picture of the tree he had taken a few years earlier.

There is also a legend of a tunnel from Sinai House to Burton Abbey, and there is a blocked-up entrance in the cellars at Sinai. Most local people firmly believe in this, but an underground tunnel seems unlikely as it would have to pass beneath the River Trent. Many tunnel legends are based not on underground passages but on 'green tunnels' through the ancient forests, the 'tunnel' being formed by the overhead boughs of the trees.

BIBLIOGRAPHY

Staffordshire Legends by Alan Gibson. published by
Churnet Valley Books 2002

The Folklore of Staffordshire by Jon Raven. pub by B T
Batsford Ltd 1978

Magic, Myth & Memories in The Peak District by Doug
Pickford. pub by Sigma leisure 1993

Earth Mysteries of the Three Shires by Doug Pickford. pub
by Churnet Valley Books 1996

Ghosts & Legends of Staffordshire & the Black Country by
David Bell. pub by Countryside Books 1994

Some Staffordshire Ghosts by Ros Prince. pub by
Staffordshire County Library 1981

Staffordshire Tales of Mystery and Murder by David Bell.
pub by Countryside Books 2005

Abbots Bromley by Marcia Alice Rice. pub by Wilding &
Sons 1939

Guide To Britain's Pagan Heritage by Dr David Clarke. Pub
by Robert Hale Ltd 1995

Supernatural Peak District by Dr David Clarke. pub by
Robert Hale Ltd 2001

THANKS and ACKNOWLEDGEMENTS

I would like to give my grateful thanks to the following people for their help: Julie Rebecca Saunt, Lesley Hextall, Bruce Braithwaite, Richard Sanders, Margaret Jones, Jacky Ayre, Ray Fallows, Barry Vallens, John Godwin, Rosemary Vanstone, K Booth, Nigel Slater and John Kay.

**More Ghost Stories from
Bradwell Books on next page**

BLACK COUNTRY - Ghost Stories

CAMBRIDGESHIRE - Ghost Stories

CHESHIRE - Ghost Stories

CORNISH COTSWOLDS - Ghost Stories

CUMBRIAN - Ghost Stories

DERBYSHIRE - Ghost Stories

KENT - Ghost Stories

LANCASHIRE - Ghost Stories

LEICESTERSHIRE - Ghost Stories

OXFORDSHIRE - Ghost Stories

SCOTTISH - Ghost Stories

SUSSEX - Ghost Stories

NORTH WALES - Ghost Stories

SOUTH WALES - Ghost Stories

YORKSHIRE - Ghost Stories

Coming Later in 2014

COTSWOLDS - Ghost Stories

ESSEX - Ghost Stories

WELSH CELEBRITY - Ghost Stories

LONDON UNDERGROUND - Ghost Stories

For more details of our books, visit our website

bradwellbooks.co.uk